Help Me Understand

What Happens When Someone in My Family Is Deaf?

Jennifer Lombardo

PowerKiDS press.

New York

Published in 2020 by The Rosen Publishing Group, Inc.
29 East 21st Street, New York, NY 10010

First Edition

Editor: Rachel Gintner
Book Design: Rachel Rising

Photo Credits: Cover, pp. 13, 15 Andrey_Popov/Shutterstock.com; pp. 4, 17 New Africa/Shutterstock.com; p. 5 Erica Smit/Shutterstock.com; p. 6 watchara phochareung/Shutterstock.com; p. 7 Bloomberg/Contributor/Getty Images; p. 9 Sean Pavone/Shutterstock.com; p.10 Monika Wisniewska/Shutterstock.com; p. 11 andras_csontos/Shutterstock.com; p. 16 Pixel-Shot/Shutterstock.com; p. 19 Scott Terrell/ASSOCIATED PRESS/Alamy Stock Photo; p. 20 pedalist/Shutterstock.com; p. 21 Monkey Business Images/Shutterstock.com; p. 22 LightField Studios/Shutterstock.com.

Library of Congress Cataloging-in-Publication Data

Names: Lombardo, Jennifer, author.
Title: What happens when someone in my family is deaf? / Jennifer Lombardo.
Description: New York : PowerKids Press, [2020] | Series: Help me understand | Includes index. | Summary: "According to the World Health Organization (WHO), more than 5 percent of the world's population has disabling hearing loss. Some people's hearing loss is mild. They can communicate through spoken language and may use a hearing aid. Some people have profound hearing loss, which most people refer to as being deaf. In this book, readers will learn the causes of deafness and the different ways in which deaf people communicate. Full-color photographs and age-appropriate text help readers understand this common condition"– Provided by publisher.
Identifiers: LCCN 2019031982 | ISBN 9781725309661 (paperback) | ISBN 9781725309685 (library binding) | ISBN 9781725309678 | ISBN 9781725309692 (ebook)
Subjects: LCSH: Deaf–Juvenile literature. | Deaf–Means of communication–Juvenile literature. | Deafness–Juvenile literature.
Classification: LCC HV2380 .L66 2020 | DDC 362.4/23–dc23
LC record available at https://lccn.loc.gov/2019031982

Manufactured in the United States of America

CPSIA Compliance Information: Batch #CS20PK. For Further Information contact Rosen Publishing, New York, New York at 1-800-237-9932.

Contents

What Does "Deaf" Mean? 4
Learning to Communicate 6
Trying to Understand 10
Making Things Accessible 12
Feeling Frustrated 14
Learning Deaf Culture 16
CODAs 18
Sticking Up for Others 20
Finding Common Ground 22
Glossary 23
Index 24
Websites 24

What Does "Deaf" Mean?

Put simply, being deaf means you can't hear most sounds. Some deaf people can hear very loud sounds, but many can't hear anything at all—that is, unless they have a **device** to help them hear. Someone can be born deaf or become deaf later in life.

Maybe you have a brother or a sister who was born deaf. Or, maybe one of your parents was born deaf or has **damage** to their hearing. No matter who it is, there are ways you can better interact with a deaf person.

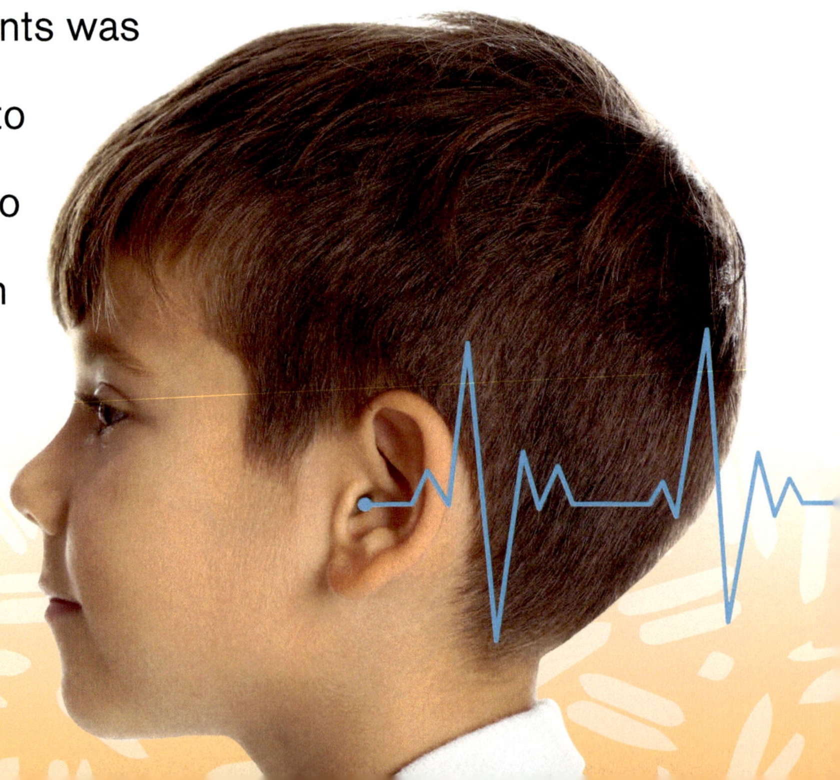

It’s important to get your hearing tested every couple of years.

Learning to Communicate

It can be hard to learn how to communicate, or share messages, with a deaf family member. You have to do things a little differently than with hearing people. You can't say their name to get their attention. You might have to tap them on the shoulder or wave your hand to get them to see you.

Many deaf people know at least two languages: a signed one and a spoken one. In the United States, most deaf people learn American Sign Language (ASL) and English.

The Alphabet in American Sign Langauge

Different countries have their own sign language, and they're not the same as their spoken languages.

If your family member knows ASL, ask them to teach you! You can talk to them more easily. You could also help them by being an **interpreter** when someone who doesn't know ASL wants to talk to them.

If your younger brother or sister is the first one in the family to be born deaf, your family should start learning ASL right away. This way, you can teach them! Babies who are deaf learn how to communicate much faster when their first language is ASL.

Think of how long it would take you to learn to speak a language just by reading it! That's what it's like for deaf people to learn English.

レンタル
カラオケ
全店営業中
歌舞伎町牧場
FACE
コミック&ネットカフェ
comics & internet cafe
aprecio
アプレシオ
新宿最大
直進30m
ハイジアB1
ダーツ
インターネット
レディースルーム
北の家族
まんが喫茶
♪エノケン流れる楽しいお店。♪
薄利多賣
炭火串焼
半兵ヱ
星のしずく
PRIVATE DINING
カラオケ
麻雀
コロッケクラブ
GRAN CYBER CAFE
グラン・サイバーカフェ
インターネット&コミック
3F カラオケの鉄人
レンタルルーム ホステル
ビリヤード&ダーツ
シミュレーションゴルフ バグース
新宿コパボウル
COPABOWL
まんが喫茶
ゲラゲラ
地域最大!!
ゲーム
メダル
クレーン
TVゲーム
カードゲーム
プリクラ
メンズサウナ
24H 年中無休
こり・こり
Pavilion
エジプト料理と和の共演
RESTAURANT
コーヒーショップ クール
無料案内所
とんかつ
ぶ
南館

Trying to Understand

Remember that if a deaf person isn't answering you, they're probably not ignoring you. They just don't know you're trying to get their attention. Try something different to let them know you want to talk to them.

Some deaf people use hearing aids or a **cochlear implant** to help them hear. This makes it easier for deaf and hearing people to speak to each other. However, not all deaf people want one of these devices, and that's OK! You can find other ways to communicate, such as writing notes or signing.

cochlear implant

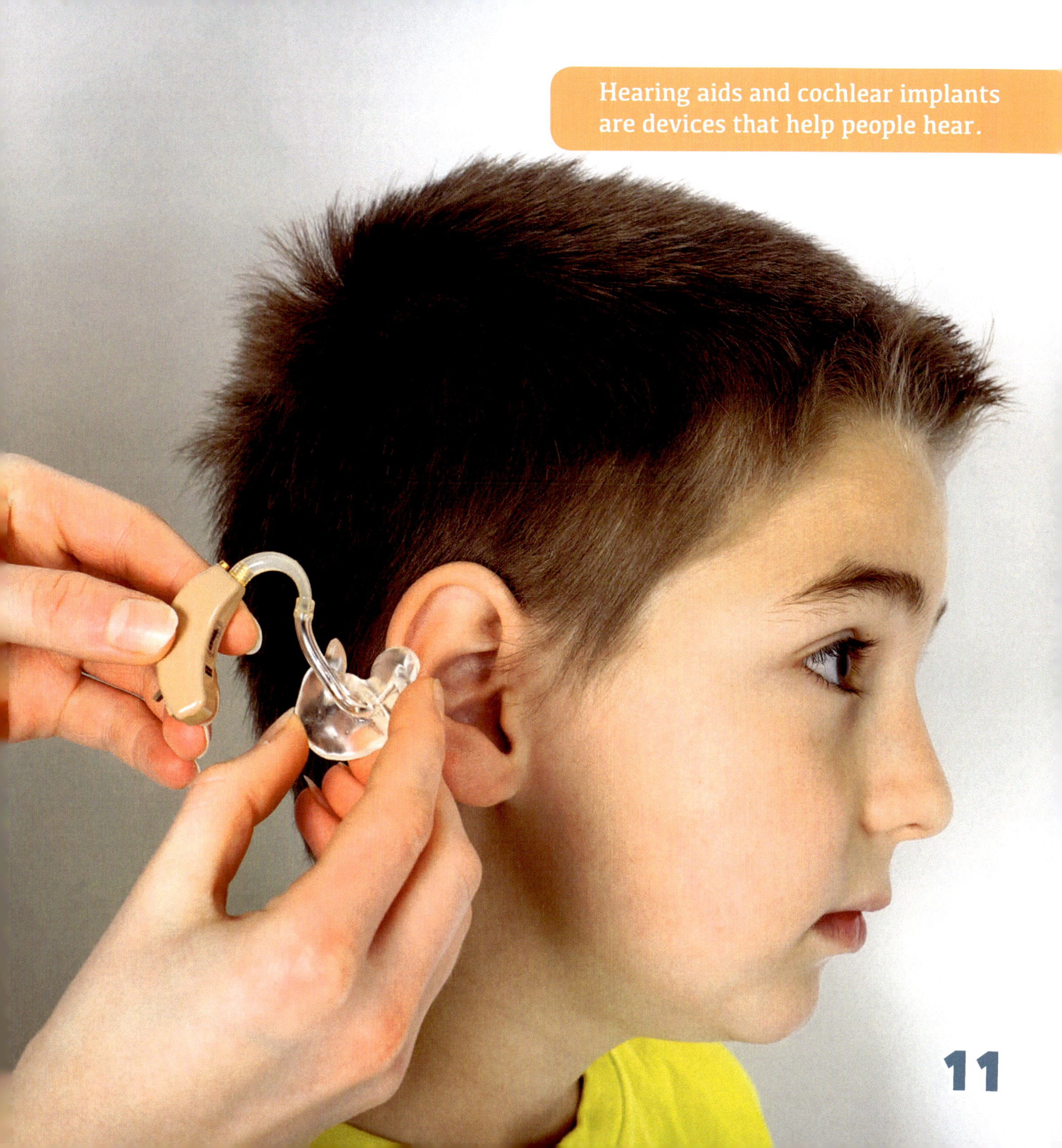

Hearing aids and cochlear implants are devices that help people hear.

Making Things Accessible

People can help their deaf family members by making things **accessible**. For example, when you watch TV together, put on the **closed captioning** so the deaf person can read what people are saying.

Some hearing people don't like closed captioning, but imagine how annoying it would be to watch the TV on mute, or soundless, all the time! That's what it's like for a deaf person. You might even find out that the closed captioning makes it easier for you to understand the show, too.

Watching TV together should be something everyone can enjoy. Sometimes that means using closed captioning.

This recipe looks great.
Can't wait to try it.

Feeling Frustrated

Sometimes you might feel like everything is about your deaf family member. You might get mad that you have to learn a new language just to talk to them. You might feel **frustrated** or **embarrassed** when they talk too loudly and people turn to look at them or you.

It's OK to have these feelings sometimes! Remember that your deaf family member isn't doing these things to frustrate you on purpose. Talking about your feelings with someone who understands is a good way to deal with your frustration.

Talking through a problem is always better than just hoping it goes away.

Learning Deaf Culture

Many people who're born deaf are active in the deaf community, which has its own **culture**. Often, these people capitalize the word "Deaf." If you have a Deaf family member or friend, you can ask them about their culture. This is a good way to learn more about someone you love.

Deaf culture has its own music, poetry, and plays. Also, some ways of behaving are different. Some things you might do with other hearing people, such as talking to someone while you're looking at something else, are rude in Deaf culture.

People are often excited to share what they love about their culture with people who are open minded.

CODAs

Just like deaf people have their own community, children of deaf adults (CODAs) have their own community. If you're a CODA, meeting other CODAs might be helpful. Sometimes it's hard for people to understand something if they haven't **experienced** it themselves.

CODAs can give each other advice and help support each other. Shared experiences help people make friends. CODAs can and do have friends who don't have deaf parents, but it can be nice to have some friends who've experienced the same things you have.

Keith Wann is a CODA. He's a hearing comedian who performs his show in ASL. An interpreter tells the hearing people in the audience what he's saying.

Sticking Up for Others

Someone who doesn't know any deaf people might be curious about what it's like to have a deaf family member. They might ask you questions that you think are rude, or they might make fun of your family member for being different. This might make you feel angry or sad.

If people do this, try to be **patient**, even though that might be hard. Explain to your friends what being deaf is like and remind them that deaf people–and their family members–have feelings, too.

Being patient and kind is the best way to help people understand that it's never OK to bully others for being deaf or for having a deaf loved one.

Finding Common Ground

It's good to remember that your deaf family member is different from you in some ways but the same as you in others. You can hear things they can't, but they might like the same movies as you or think the same jokes are funny.

Being deaf doesn't mean someone isn't smart or fun to talk to. Treat your deaf family member just like you treat everyone else. You can learn things from each other and be friends as well as family!

Glossary

accessible: Easy to use or understand.

closed captioning: A written version of the spoken part of a TV show, program, or movie.

cochlear implant: An electronic device inserted into part of the ear called the cochlea. It sends sounds directly to the hearing nerve, unlike a hearing aid, which just makes sounds louder.

culture: The beliefs and ways of life of a certain group of people.

damage: Loss or harm.

device: A tool used for a certain purpose.

embarrassed: Feeling shame.

experience: To see or do something.

frustrated: Feeling angered or let down.

interpreter: A person who interprets, or changes one language into another so two people can communicate, or share messages.

patient: Able to remain calm when waiting for a long time or when dealing with problems.

Index

A
American Sign Language (ASL), 6, 8, 18
attention, 6, 10

B
babies, 8

C
closed captioning, 12
cochlear implant, 10, 11
CODAs, 18
culture, 16

D
damage, 4
devices, 4, 10, 11

E
English, 6, 8

F
feelings, 14, 20
friend, 16, 18, 20, 22
frustration, 16, 18

H
hearing aids, 10, 11

I
interpreter, 8, 18

L
languages, 6, 7, 8, 14

P
parent, 4

S
sounds, 4

T
TV, 12

U
United States, 6

W
Wann, Keith, 18

Websites

Due to the changing nature of Internet links, PowerKids Press has developed an online list of websites related to the subject of this book. This site is updated regularly. Please use this link to access the list: www.powerkidslinks.com/HMU/deaf